PRIMATES IN THE ZOO

BY ROLAND SMITH

Photographs by
WILLIAM MUÑOZ

**THE NEW ZOO
THE MILLBROOK PRESS
BROOKFIELD, CT.**

Library of Congress Cataloging-in-Publication Data

Smith, Roland, 1951–
Primates in the zoo / by Roland Smith ; photographs
by William Muñoz.

p.   cm. — (The New zoo)
Includes bibliographical references and index.
Summary: Describes the various species of primates and their care
in the zoo, discussing their social behavior, communication, diet,
and breeding in captivity.
ISBN 1-56294-210-7 (lib. bdg.)
1. Primates—Juvenile literature.   2. Primates—Handling—Juvenile
literature.   3. Zoo animals—Juvenile literature.   [1. Primates.
2. Zoo animals.]   I. Muñoz, William, ill.   II. Title.   III. Series:
Smith, Roland, 1951–   New zoo.
SF408.6.P74S55   1992
636'.98—dc20   91-46968   CIP   AC r92

Contents

The author and photographer wish to
thank the following organizations and
individuals for their help with this book:

Zoo Atlanta,
Busch Gardens of Florida,
Brookfield Zoo, Cincinnati Zoo,
Duke Primate Center,
Knoxville Zoo, Phoenix Zoo,
Lincoln Park Zoo, Lowry Park Zoo,
Point Defiance Zoo and Aquarium,
Reid Park Zoo, St. Louis Zoo,
Woodland Park Zoo,
Hunter Clarke, Peg Clarke,
Barbara Coffman,
Margaret Gaspari,
John Houck,
Michael Roydon,
Frank Slavens,
and Jim Tuten.

Introduction

Years ago, before many of us understood how we were harming the earth and its wildlife, a zoo's main function was to entertain and amuse its human visitors. Today, many of the animals kept in zoos are not there for our entertainment. They are there because it is no longer safe for them in the wild.

Zoos today are a little like Noah's Ark—"lifeboats" for saving animals from extinction. On the ship with the animals are their human keepers. During the voyage, the keepers do everything they can to make the animals comfortable in their artificial environment.

While the keepers are caring for the animals, they are also looking for "dry land"—habitats that might be suitable for a few of the animals on the ship. In Noah's time, after the flood, there were very few people on the earth and an abundance of wilderness areas. Today, there are many people and very few wilderness areas. It is no longer easy to find undisturbed land where animals can live in peace.

The books in this series are about what happens to the animals inside the zoo ark during their stay—how they got there, how they are cared for, and what their future is.

CHAPTER II
094-C2-93

Of all the animals kept in zoos, monkeys and apes may be the most popular. Perhaps they are so fascinating to us because when we look at them, we almost see ourselves. They move a lot like us, their hands and faces are similar to ours, they nurture their babies like we do, and they have the ability to use tools. In fact, there are so many similarities among monkeys, apes, and humans that they are scientifically classified together as *primates*. People, or *Homo sapiens*, are human primates.

There are 180 different species of primates in the world. Of these, nearly half are in danger of extinction. In this book we will go behind the scenes for a close look at how we care for our distant relatives in the zoo environment.

What Primates Are Like

Before we look at how primates are cared for in zoos, we must understand at least some aspects of their behavior. Keepers always try to see the world as an animal sees it, so they can set up a successful zoo environment. For example, they study how primates communicate and how they interact socially.

How primates communicate • Primates are able to make a wide range of sounds, but they do not have a language system like ours. How do they communicate?

Primates are experts in *nonverbal* communication—ways of communicating other than written and spoken words. Humans also communicate nonverbally, but because we rely on words, we are less aware of our nonverbal communication.

Smiling, frowning, clenching our fists, and nodding or shaking our heads—all are examples of human nonverbal communication. Even our posture (the way we hold our head and the position of our shoulders) communicates nonverbally. But probably the most effective nonverbal communicators are our eyes. If we are talking to someone and they start to look around the room, we know that they are probably not listening to us. When we want to know if someone approves of what we are doing, we look into their eyes.

You can get a better idea of how primates communicate by performing a little experiment. This experiment can be done with a friend, your family, or classmates. Pick an hour out of the day when you will communicate nonverbally only. Do not use any written or spoken words. You can use touch, gestures, grunts, facial expressions—anything but words.

Several interesting things should happen during the experiment. You might be surprised by how much you are able to communicate and understand without using words. You will find yourself paying much closer attention to your family, classmates, or friends than normal. This is because without speech, you *have* to look at them. With speech, you can look away and still understand what is being said because you can hear the words. The other thing that you'll probably notice is how much you must exaggerate your facial expressions and gestures because you don't have confidence that people will understand you.

The next time you go to the zoo, watch how primates communicate. You might notice that a primate's nonverbal communication is much more subtle than your exaggerated version—the primate's facial expressions, for example, are not so obvious to the human eye. In fact, primate communication is so subtle that even scientists have a difficult time understanding it.

Primates, like this lion-tailed macaque,
are experts in nonverbal communication.

Social behavior • Most primates live in social groups. The size of the groups varies depending on the species. For instance, orangutans live in small groups of three or four animals. Baboons often form groups of more than a hundred animals. A group provides security for the individual animal because there are more ears, eyes, and noses to detect danger. There is also greater power in a large group. The size of the group makes a predator such as a lion think twice before it attacks.

In every group, including humans, there is what is known as a "social hierarchy." To understand social hierarchy, imagine a tall ladder with a single person or animal standing on each rung. The animals on the ladder all belong to one group. An animal on a higher rung has a higher "rank" than an animal on the lower rung.

Think of the social groups you are in. In families there are brothers, sisters, and parents. Older children are usually on higher rungs than younger children. Parents are on a higher rung than all of the children. They are the leaders of the group. Parents tell children when to go to bed, what to eat, and when to be home. At school, teachers are on a higher rung than their students. They help the students by teaching them, giving them assignments, and by establishing classroom rules. Even among your friends, there is probably a social hierarchy, where one person takes the lead and makes the important decisions.

The next time you go to the zoo, ask what time the primates are fed. Social hierarchy is easiest to observe during feeding times. You'll see that the higher-ranking animals usually get to eat before the lower-ranking animals. By understanding how the group works, keepers can make sure that all the primates get their fair share.

The social structure of a primate group changes from time to time. In the zoo, keepers pay very close attention to these changes. One reason for change is that as a monkey or an ape matures, or grows up, it tries to move up the ladder and take the place of older animals on higher rungs. Another reason for change in the zoo hierarchy is that primates come and go. When a new primate is introduced to a group, the organization of the group changes. Any change in the social group affects how the keeper takes care of the group.

In this book, we will discuss the care of primates in the zoo.

Caring for Primates in the Zoo

Primate care in a zoo environment involves much more than providing food and an exhibit area. Baby primates, in particular, often require special attention in zoos. This chapter discusses the special needs of primates in captivity.

Exhibit design • Primate exhibits come in all shapes and sizes. Some are made out of concrete and glass; others are made out of wire mesh. Many are surrounded by water or dry moats (deep, wide ditches). For an exhibit to "work," it must be large enough for the animals, escape-proof, safe for the animals and keepers, easy to manage the animals in, enjoyable to look at, and easy to clean.

Years ago, zoos built rather plain and bare primate exhibits. Sometimes these exhibits were as simple as a concrete or tile box with wire mesh in front of it. These "primate boxes" were easy to clean and inexpensive, but there was nothing for monkeys and apes to do in them. Primates are very intelligent and need to interact with their environment as well as with each other. Without some stimulation, they become bored and can develop behavioral and physical problems.

The water around this island zoo exhibit
helps keep the primates from escaping.

Fortunately, these bare exhibits can be fixed up. Branches, logs, ropes, and bars can be added for the primates to swing and climb on. Straw can be put on the floor for them to pick through and build nests out of. Toys, including balls, cardboard boxes, barrels, and burlap bags, can be put in for them to play with. Adding these things can make the exhibit more difficult to clean, but most zoos believe that it is the least they can do to make their monkeys and apes more comfortable.

Most primate exhibits have some type of holding area. A holding area can be as simple as a wooden box with a sliding door in it, or as complicated as a series of tunnels leading to larger holding areas that are separate from the exhibit.

Holding areas are very important tools for managing primates in zoos. They are used to hold primates while the keeper is cleaning the exhibit. Primates that are injured or sick are often put in holding areas until they are well again. When an individual monkey or ape is put in a holding area, the keeper can make sure it gets the medication or special diet it needs without the other primates interfering. Primates will also often be put in holding areas at night to sleep.

Over the last several years, zoos have started to build more naturalistic exhibits for monkeys and apes—surroundings that are more like the animals' habitats in the wild. Not only are these exhibits better for the primates, they also give the zoo visitor a chance to see how the animal functions in a natural setting.

As beautiful as some naturalistic exhibits are, they do present some special problems for keepers. Aside from being more difficult to take care of (because of the live plants), it is sometimes hard to tell how escape-proof they are until after the primate is in the exhibit. When building a new exhibit, keepers try to think of every possible way an animal might try to escape. Primates put in a new exhibit are watched very closely.

If there is a way out of an exhibit, a monkey or an ape will find it. One zoo built a beautiful outdoor exhibit with a water moat around it. It looked very natural, with live trees, plants, grass, streams, and large pools of water. On opening day a group of reporters and camera operators came to film the opening for the evening news. When they arrived, they found the monkeys sitting in the visitor area admiring their own exhibit—as if *they* were the zoo visitors! The news crew didn't film the exhibit that day. Instead, they filmed the keepers catching the monkeys and fixing the exhibit so they couldn't escape again!

Escapes • Primate escapes are rare in zoos, but monkeys and apes do get out from time to time. How keepers respond to these emergencies depends on the type of primate and where the animal goes when it escapes.

An exhibit is a primate's home. In the exhibit the animal feels comfortable and knows what to expect. Outside its exhibit, a monkey or an ape may become frightened and confused. As we learned earlier, primates are experts at reading nonverbal language. Because of this, keepers try to stay calm when they discover a loose monkey or ape. They realize that if they panic, the primate might panic also, and this will make it more difficult to catch.

If a primate gets loose inside a building, keepers try to make sure that it doesn't get out of the building. Containing the animal in a small space is the first step in capturing it. The keeper may use food to lure the monkey or ape back into its exhibit. If this doesn't work, the keeper may have to net the animal and carry it back to the exhibit. Obviously, using a net will not work with larger apes, such as chimpanzees, gorillas, or orangutans. If food fails to tempt an ape back into its cage, a tranquilizer dart or blowgun may have to be used to tranquilize the animal.

A primate that escapes from an outdoor exhibit is much more difficult to catch. Not only is the primate in an open area, but the keeper also has to worry about the potential danger to zoo visitors. For their size, primates are very strong. They are not usually aggressive toward humans, but if a zoo visitor were to get too close or try to touch it, the primate could injure the person. As with indoor escapes, food is used to lure the escaped primate back into its exhibit, or into an indoor area where it can be captured more easily.

Handling primates • Primates are not pets and do not like to be handled. They have powerful arms and legs, and large teeth and strong jaws that they will not hesitate to use if they feel threatened. However, zoo primates need to be handled when getting medical checkups or treatments or when they have to be moved.

Small primates, such as marmosets and squirrel monkeys,

are usually caught while they are in their nest boxes and handled with a gloved hand.

Larger primates are more difficult to handle because of their size and strength. Nets are often used to catch them, and while still in the net, the animal will be injected with a tranquilizer.

Apes such as chimpanzees, gorillas, and orangutans are sometimes darted in their holding areas. A tranquilizer dart is fired from a special pistol, rifle, or blowgun. The dart itself is a syringe with a needle on the end of it. When the dart hits the animal, a tranquilizing drug is injected, and within about 15 minutes the primate becomes calm enough for keepers to handle without risking injury.

Another device used to tranquilize primates is the "extension syringe." An extension syringe is a long pole with a syringe and needle on the end of it. With this type of syringe the veterinarian can stand at a distance (outside the holding area) and inject the ape with tranquilizer.

Another way of restraining a primate is with a squeeze cage. A squeeze cage contains one wall that can be moved inward and trap the animal so that it can't move and injure itself while getting an injection. Most squeeze cages have a hand crank for moving the wall. As soon as the primate has gotten its injection, the wall is pulled back again. Often primates have to pass through a squeeze cage to get to their holding area. In this way they become used to the squeeze cage, which makes it easier to catch them in it.

A zookeeper removes a siamang from a portable squeeze cage after the animal has been tranquilized.

Feeding time • Among the foods that primates eat in the wild are fruits, nuts, vegetables, leaves, seeds, small mammals, birds, mushrooms, eggs, tree bark, and wood pulp. In the zoo they are fed as wide a variety of food as possible. Most primates seem particularly fond of fruit, with vegetables running a close second. Another item fed to primates in zoos is monkey chow, a commercially prepared dry food made from corn, wheat, soybean, whey, animal fat, alfalfa meal, beef pulp, and fish meat. These ingredients are mixed together, and vitamins and minerals are added. The mixture is then dried and made into small, hard biscuits.

Monkeys and apes are often put in a holding area in the morning to be fed their first meal. While they are eating, the keeper cleans their exhibit. After the exhibit has been cleaned, the keeper spreads their next meal around the exhibit and hides some of it so the primates will have to look for it. In this way the monkeys and apes have to forage for their food as they do in the wild.

The diet is carefully controlled. Primates are not as active in zoos as they are in the wild and therefore don't burn as many calories. If a primate is gaining too much weight, keepers will cut back on its food. Obesity—too much weight—can cause many health problems in zoo primates, just as it can in humans.

During feeding time, keepers watch the primates closely to make sure that disputes over food don't get out of hand and that everyone in the group gets a share. If there are problems within the group, keepers will sometimes separate individual primates during feeding.

A young hand-reared chimpanzee enjoys a drink.

Baby primates • When a baby primate is born, it is totally dependent on its mother for all of its needs. The mother feeds it, cleans it, keeps it warm, and protects it from danger. Almost from the moment of birth, the baby has the ability to cling to its mother so that she is free to travel with the group. In some primates, like gibbons and marmosets, the father shares the burden of carrying the baby.

As the baby grows older, it begins to interact with other members of the group. Under the watchful eyes of its parents, the baby plays with other youngsters and with its older brothers and sisters. These play sessions are very important to the baby's development. By playing and interacting with other primates, the baby learns how to function in the group. Juvenile (young) primates also learn how to treat babies during these play sessions. Zoos usually allow juvenile monkeys and apes to stay with their parents through one or two births. By playing with infants, juvenile primates learn how to care for their own babies when they are old enough to reproduce. Without this experience, primates often have problems rearing their own young. This is one reason that most zoos are reluctant to *hand rear* baby primates. This means that the baby is taken from its mother and raised by humans.

Unfortunately, there are times when hand rearing cannot be avoided. Baby primates are sometimes taken from their mothers because they have been injured, or because there is a threat of injury from other primates in the exhibit. A baby's mother might be injured or die, leaving an orphan whose only chance of survival is to be hand reared. Sometimes a mother may simply refuse to take care of her baby.

Zoos know that hand rearing a baby primate is a poor substitute for its natural mother. The people who work in the zoo nursery can provide the proper food and care, but only the baby's parents can provide what it needs to develop into a *psychologically* healthy adult—one that functions well in its social group. To help with the baby's development, zoos will often try to find another baby primate to rear with it. This may mean shipping the baby to a zoo that is hand rearing another baby primate, or having that baby primate shipped in from the other zoo.

If a suitable cage mate is not available, the nursery staff must provide all the social contact that is necessary for the infant's development. This type of human/animal interaction is called *imprinting*.

When baby primates are born, they "imprint" on their natural mothers. The mother becomes the baby's security. By watching her, the baby learns the rules of survival. Imprinting is one way a chimpanzee learns that it is a chimpanzee, and we learn that we are humans. Imprinting helps the youngster grow into a well-adjusted adolescent and adult, making it possible for the animal to fit easily into the social organization of its particular animal group.

When a baby primate has to be taken from its mother at a young age and raised by humans, it may imprint on humans. As the baby matures, this can cause problems, especially when the

A baby lemur clings to its mother's back.

time comes for it to be introduced to animals of its own kind. Every type of animal species has different rules by which it lives. These rules are usually learned when very young, and the change from one set of rules to another can be very difficult.

To understand this, imagine for a moment that you were adopted by a group of gorillas when you were a baby. For the first years of your life you were carried through the forest by your gorilla mother. You slept outside, you played gorilla games, and you foraged for food in the forest. Then, when you were five years old, you were taken away from the gorillas and put back with humans. In this new society you found that there was a spoken language and that you were expected to wear clothes. Food was paid for at a grocery store, and this strange food was eaten with forks and knives. Instead of sleeping on the ground in the forest, you were made to sleep on a bed in a house. Almost everything would be different from what you were used to. It would take a long time to learn a new way of behaving.

In the zoo nursery, imprinting on humans cannot be totally avoided, but its effects can be lessened by letting baby animals socialize with species of their own or similar kind. Another way to reduce the effects of imprinting is to put the baby with others of its own kind as soon as possible.

Primate medicine • Zoo primates can get many of the same diseases that humans do. In most zoos, if a keeper thinks he or she is coming down with an illness, the keeper will wear a surgical mask to prevent the spread of germs.

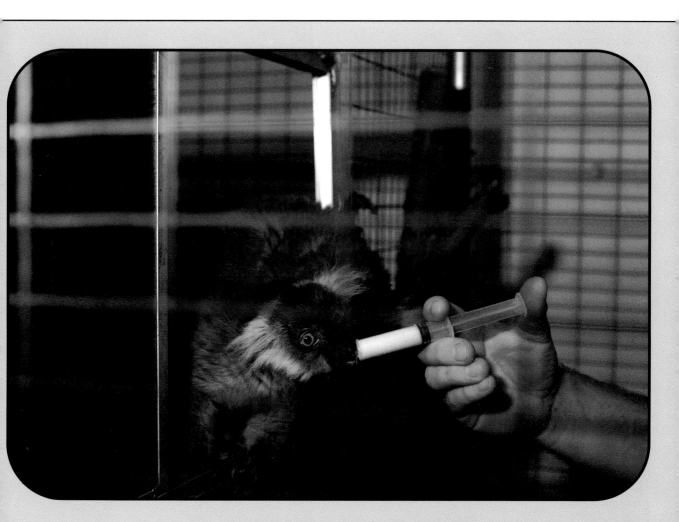

To stay healthy, primates need to get
their vitamins. This young lemur gets
his mixed in a tasty drink.

Because primates are difficult to treat when they are sick, keepers try to make sure the animals stay healthy by providing a clean environment, good food, and a stable social group where fighting is kept to a minimum.

A sick monkey or ape is usually kept separate from the group so that it can be watched closely and given medication. Often the medication doesn't taste good. To get the primate to take its medication, keepers mix it with a treat the primate enjoys, such as fruit, orange juice, or even ice cream.

Most zoos *quarantine* new primates before they are put in with other primates. This means that the animal is isolated, or kept away from the other primates. This is one way to prevent disease from being brought in from the outside. A quarantine period may last from 30 to 60 days, depending on the zoo's policy. During quarantine the new primate is examined for signs of any health problems, such as infections. Before the new primate can go in with the others, it must be in perfect health.

In the next two chapters, we will introduce a few of the primate species commonly kept in zoos. The primate routines that we discuss are typical of how most primates are cared for in captivity.

Monkeys in the Zoo Ark

Of the 180 species of primates, most are classified as monkeys. Monkeys are found throughout the tropics and come in all sizes and colors. The mandrill baboon from Africa weighs up to 55 pounds (25 kilograms), the average weight of an eight-year-old human. Compare this with the delicate pygmy marmoset from South America, which weighs a mere 2 ounces (0.06 kilogram), a little less than a mouse. Some monkeys (the golden lion tamarin from the jungles of Brazil, for example), have brightly colored fur. Other primates, such as baboons, have drably colored fur, ranging from brown to gray.

Lemurs • There are 16 species of lemurs. In the wild they are found only on the islands of Madagascar and Comoro, which are off the southeastern coast of Africa. Lemurs are one of the more unusual-looking animals found in zoos and are the oldest living primates on earth. They are called *prosimians*, which means "before primates." The island of Madagascar separated from the African continent millions of years ago. Because of their isolation, the primates living on this island evolved differently than the primates living on the continent of Africa.

Lemurs vary greatly in size. The indri lemur weighs over 20 pounds (9 kilograms) and is the largest prosimian on earth; the mouse lemur may be the smallest prosimian, weighing less than 2 ounces (0.06 kilogram). Unlike all other primates, many lemurs are nocturnal, meaning that they are most active at night.

Probably the most common lemur found in zoos is the ring-tailed lemur. Ring-tailed lemurs differ from other lemurs partly in that they spend as much time on the ground as they do in trees. Most zoos keep ring-tailed lemurs in large social groups of a dozen or more animals. They are a very hardy species and in temperate climates can be kept in outdoor enclosures. In the wild, ring-tailed lemurs eat fruits, flowers, and leaves. In captivity, they are fed a variety of fruits and vegetables. Keepers generally spread their food throughout an exhibit so that the lemurs will forage for their food as they do in the wild.

Ring-tailed lemurs have a single baby after a gestation period (pregnancy) of about 130 days. For the first two weeks the youngster clings to the mother's abdomen. After this, the baby rides on the mother's back. At six months of age the young lemur is old enough to be on its own. Ring-tailed lemurs are able to reproduce at about 18 months.

Other types of lemurs are kept in indoor exhibits. Because they are active at night, zoos often reverse their day-night cycle. During the day, when keepers and visitors are there to observe them, their exhibit is kept darkened or red lights are used. During the night, their exhibit is brightly lit, which encourages them to sleep.

In the wild, mouse lemurs are believed to eat primarily insects and some fruits. In the zoo, they are fed a variety of fruits and vegetables, as well as mealworms and crickets. They generally live in the tops of the tallest trees, where larger lemurs cannot go. They make nests in tree cavities and line them with dried leaves. In the zoo, they are given small nest boxes to sleep and hide in.

Mouse lemurs have two or three young after a gestation period of about 60 days. The young are no bigger than your thumb and cling to their mother for the first two weeks of life. They are able to walk when they are three weeks old, and at two months they are totally independent of their mother. Mouse lemurs can produce young when they are seven to ten months old.

Because their habitat is disappearing and because they are also killed for food, lemurs are rare in the wild. Hunters use sharpened sticks, traps, snares, slings and stones, and blowguns. They also cut down trees and take the small lemurs from their nests. The ground-dwelling ring-tailed lemur is sometimes hunted with dogs.

Marmosets and tamarins • Marmosets and tamarins are among the smallest and most beautiful primates in the world. They range in color from black to bright orange. Many of them, like the golden lion tamarin, have "manes" of long hair around their heads. There are 35 species living in the tropical rain forests of South America and Panama. The main

One unusual lemur found on the island of Madagascar is the aye-aye (pronounced I-I).

Because marmosets like climbing, their cages need to have lots of perches, ropes, and branches.

difference between tamarins and marmosets is that tamarins have larger canine teeth. In the wild, both species live in small family groups consisting of an adult pair and four or five off-spring of different ages.

In zoos, marmosets are generally kept indoors. Their cages are filled with perches and branches for climbing. The floor is covered with straw, sawdust, wood shavings, or bark strippings. This floor covering not only gives the marmosets a chance to pick through ground cover as they would in the wild, but it also acts as a cushion should a primate slip and fall while climbing or jumping from branch to branch.

Heated nest boxes are provided for marmosets to hide and sleep in. The nest boxes are also used to catch the animals. To catch a marmoset, the keeper simply goes into the exhibit early in the morning before the marmoset wakes up and closes the nest box door. Because of their small size, marmosets can be handled safely with a gloved hand.

In the wild, marmosets eat fruits and insects. When fruit is scarce, some marmoset species have learned how to tap trees and drink tree sap. In captivity, their main diet consists of bananas, apples, pears, oranges, tomatoes, and figs. Additions to this diet may include day-old chick legs, pieces of cooked chicken, grapes, yogurt, cream cheese, sunflower seeds, pea-nuts, canned dog or cat food, and hard-boiled eggs. Their diet is supplemented with vitamin D. Because most captive marmo-sets are housed indoors, they do not have sunlight to help them produce this essential vitamin. Without it, bone problems can develop (especially in young animals), which can cause deformities and even lead to death.

In the wild, 25 percent of the marmoset's time is spent foraging for food. In captivity, live crickets and mealworms are released in the cage so that the marmoset can forage for food. Many zoos have automatic cricket dispensers. The crickets are able to crawl out of the dispenser at will. As in the wild, the zoo marmoset never knows when or where a cricket is going to appear.

Marmosets have two or three young after a gestation period of around 150 days. Unlike other primates, male marmosets take an active role in raising the young. They often carry the babies on their backs, returning them to the female when it is time for them to be fed. When the babies are older, they in turn help care for their mother's next litter. In this way, young marmosets learn how to care for infants even before they are old enough to have babies of their own.

Baboons • Baboons are found throughout Africa. One thing that sets them apart from other monkeys is the size and organization of their "troops." It is not unusual for a troop to have more than 100 animals in it, and there have been reports of troops as large as 300 or 400. Baboons are probably the most social of all primates. In fact, their survival often depends on the stability of their social structure.

In the wild, troops consist of a core group of adult females, their babies, and juveniles. Older males act as guards, protecting the troop from dangerous predators. When it comes to defending the troop, these males are courageous and very aggressive. Because baboons look up from what they are doing every few seconds, it is very hard for a predator to surprise them.

Baboons eat just about anything they can find. This includes plants, insects, and even young lambs and calves. In the zoo, baboons are fed fruits, vegetables, and monkey chow. Because they are ground foragers, their food is generally spread around their exhibit.

Zoo baboons are kept in relatively small groups of a dozen or so animals. The size of the troop depends on the size of the exhibit. Many zoos keep their baboons outdoors, often on island exhibits surrounded by water. Like most monkeys, baboons are capable of swimming, but they don't like the water.

Because baboons are large and aggressive, keepers generally do not go into the exhibit when the baboons are in it. If the animals have to be handled, they are tranquilized while in the holding area or in a squeeze cage.

Females give birth to a single youngster after a gestation period of six to seven months. One thing keepers have to watch for after a baboon gives birth is "kidnapping." Older, more dominant females without babies will sometimes take the babies of younger mothers. This can put the baby in danger, because the kidnapper generally doesn't have any milk to feed it. To get the baby back to its mother, keepers may lure the kidnapper into a holding area. There they may try coaxing her to give up the baby or distracting her with food until she puts it down. Then the baby can be returned to its mother.

Baboon mothers have to watch their babies to prevent other females from kidnapping them.

In the wild, baboons still exist in fairly large numbers, although these numbers have declined in recent years because of habitat loss. Baboons have a habit of raiding farms and killing livestock. For this reason, farmers and ranchers often shoot them to protect their crops and animals.

The most threatened baboon is the beautiful mandrill. In its home in West Africa the meat of the mandrill is highly prized by the local population. Dried and smoked mandrill meat is commonly found in the markets there. Because of this, the mandrill population is rapidly disappearing, and the mandrill will no doubt become an endangered species within the next few years.

Apes in the Zoo Ark

The apes are humankind's closest living relatives. We all know the difference between human and nonhuman primates, but what's the difference between apes and monkeys? For one thing, apes do not have tails; monkeys do. Apes also have arms that are generally longer than their legs.

There are two groups in the ape family. The lesser apes include siamangs and gibbons; the great apes include chimpanzees, gorillas, and orangutans.

Gibbons and siamangs • There are six species of gibbons. There is only one species of siamang. Gibbons range in color from black to brown to pale blond. Siamangs are black. Gibbons and siamangs are very closely related. The main difference between them is that the siamang is larger than the gibbon. Gibbons are found throughout Southeast Asia, but siamangs are found only in Sumatra and on the Malay Peninsula.

Gibbons and siamangs live in the tropical rain forest in small family groups consisting of a mother, a father, and as many as three offspring, usually spaced about two years apart. Both species have throat pouches that they are able to inflate when they make sounds. Their main call is a beautiful, haunting "whooop-whooop-whoooo . . ." that can be heard for miles in the forest. This distinctive call can often be heard at the zoo early in the morning and again at dusk, just before the sun goes down.

Siamangs and gibbons may be the most acrobatic and agile of the primates. They swing through the treetops with great speed and grace. At the top of their swing, just as they let go of a branch with one hand, they catch the next branch with the other hand. This motion is called *brachiation* (break-ee-A-shun), which means "swinging by the arms." Siamangs and gibbons are able to travel as much as 45 feet (about 14 meters) from one tree branch to another, and when they are brachiating rapidly through the forest, they spend more time suspended in midair than they do touching branches. Because of their speed, it is nearly impossible for predators such as leopards to catch them.

In the zoo, siamangs and gibbons are kept in large enclosures with branches, bars, and ropes that allow them to brachiate freely. They may be kept in either indoor or outdoor exhibits. If kept outdoors, they must be brought inside whenever it gets very cold.

Gibbons and siamangs are fed a variety of fruits and vegetables, hard-boiled eggs, and a small amount of meat. As with other primates, their exhibit is often sprinkled with sunflower seeds to give them an opportunity to forage on the ground.

Females give birth to a single baby after a gestation period of around 220 days. The babies weigh about 1½ pounds (0.7 kilogram) at birth. Their fingers and toes are very strong, and they are able to hold on to their mother's fur from the moment of birth. The mother carries her infant clinging to her lower abdomen. With its long arms, the baby can reach almost all the way around its mother's waist. While swinging through the trees, the mother will tuck her knees under the infant to protect it from falling.

Even though gibbons and siamangs are difficult to catch or kill, their numbers are declining. This is because the hardwood forests in which they live are being cut down.

Chimpanzees • Chimpanzees are found in the forests of Africa, from Gambia and the lower Congo River in the west to the shores of Lake Victoria in the east. They live in social groups of 25 to 80 animals, although this large group may break up into smaller "bands" numbering just a few animals each.

In the wild, chimps are reported to feed on more than 50 types of fruits and 30 types of leaves and buds. In addition to this, they have been known to kill and eat bushbuck (small antelope), pigs, young baboons, and colobus monkeys. In captivity a typical diet for an adult male may include a quart (or a liter) of milk mixed with vitamins; some oranges, apples, and bananas; a head of lettuce; a quarter head of cabbage; some carrots and pieces of celery; half a pound (about a quarter of a kilogram) of grapes; a few potatoes; and a handful of monkey

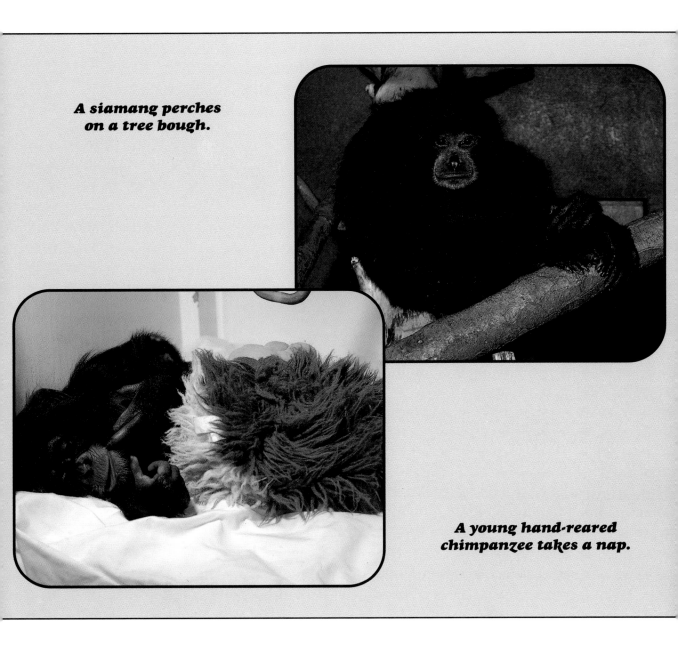

**A siamang perches
on a tree bough.**

**A young hand-reared
chimpanzee takes a nap.**

chow. Of course, this diet varies from zoo to zoo and also depends on the condition of the chimpanzee being fed.

Females weigh about 90 pounds (40 kilograms); males are slightly heavier, weighing about 110 pounds (50 kilograms). For their size, they are very powerful. In a test of strength, a female chimp was able to pull a stationary object that weighed 1,260 pounds (572 kilograms) with both hands. In contrast, seven football players were tested, and the most any one of them was able to pull with both hands was 377 pounds (171 kilograms).

In zoos, chimpanzees are kept in small groups consisting of a dominant male, several adult females, and offspring of various ages. Zoos often provide their chimp groups with both indoor and outdoor cages. Outdoor exhibits are usually surrounded by water and have structures that provide shade for the chimps. Indoor exhibits are usually equipped with shatterproof viewing windows made of glass at least 2 inches (5 centimeters) thick. Despite the strength of the glass, keepers must be careful to keep hard, pointed objects out of the cage so the chimps can't break the windows.

Both indoor and outdoor enclosures have climbing structures made out of wood, metal bars, and ropes. There are also platforms at various heights on which the chimps can rest or sleep. Most zoos cover the floors of their exhibits with straw or wood shavings so the chimps will have something to pick through. The floor covering is also used by the chimps as nesting material.

Female chimpanzees are able to reproduce when they are about nine years old. They usually give birth to one baby after a gestation period of about 225 days. The youngster is dependent on the mother for the first two years of life.

Gorillas • Gorillas are found only in Africa. There are three types: the eastern lowland gorilla, the western lowland gorilla, and the mountain gorilla. Of the three, the eastern lowland gorilla is thought to be the largest, with males weighing up to 400 pounds (about 180 kilograms) and females averaging 250 pounds (nearly 115 kilograms). The mountain gorilla has longer hair than the lowland gorilla to keep it warm in the cool mountain air. Mature male gorillas acquire a broad "saddle" of white or silver fur across their backs, and because of this they are called "silverbacks."

In the wild, gorillas live in small groups of 5 to 30 animals. The groups usually consist of a dominant silverback male, adult females, younger males and females, and infants.

Despite their size and strength, gorillas are generally very peaceful and will not attack unless they are provoked. Gorillas spend most of their time on the ground, although they do climb trees in search of food or to make nests for the night.

Like chimpanzees, gorillas are kept in outdoor and indoor enclosures equipped with structures for climbing, nest material, and sometimes sturdy toys like large "unbreakable" plastic barrels to keep them occupied.

Gorillas are fed a diet similar to that of chimpanzees.

Keepers feed them as often as five times a day, with each gorilla receiving a total of 20 to 25 pounds (9 to 11 kilograms) of food a day.

Females give birth to one youngster after a gestation period of around 260 days. The youngster stays with its mother for up to three years.

Gorillas are rapidly disappearing in the wild, mainly because of habitat loss and poaching. Poaching is the illegal killing of a protected animal. In most of their range gorillas are protected, but this legal protection hasn't completely stopped the slaughter. Poachers continue to shoot gorillas and set snares for them. Gorillas are also killed in snares set for other animals. Field biologists have found dead gorillas with their hands cut off. Poachers sell the hands to private collectors.

Orangutans • Orangutans live in the Southeast Asian jungles of Borneo and Sumatra. The people there refer to the orangutan as the "man of the woods." Orangutans are primarily tree dwellers, traveling on the ground only when they have to. In the wild they eat fruits, leaves, the inner bark from trees, palm leaves, and bamboo shoots. They are also thought to eat a number of insects, including termites. Male orangutans have a throat pouch like that of the siamangs and gibbons, which they are able to inflate to make a distinctive call. Both males and females are covered with long red hair, which makes them look bigger than they actually are. Males weigh about 250 pounds (about 112 kilograms); the much smaller females weigh only about 100 pounds (45 kilograms).

Despite their size and strength, gorillas are generally very peaceful and will not attack unless provoked.

The population of orangutans in the wild is getting smaller, but they breed well in captivity.

Adult male orangutans are thought to lead solitary lives in the wild, only starting up contact with other orangutans during breeding season. Female orangutans, on the other hand, are usually accompanied by one or more of their offspring.

In zoos, orangutans are kept much like other great apes, in both indoor and outdoor enclosures. Their enclosures, however, may have more structures for climbing. Despite their solitary nature, male orangutans seem to get along fine in an exhibit with one or more females. Adult male orangutans are not usually kept together because they will fight and injure each other.

The female gives birth to a single baby after a gestation period of around 275 days. The infant will stay with its mother for up to three years.

It is uncertain how many orangutans are left in the wild, but our best guess is fewer than 10,000. Their decline has been caused by deforestation and the pet and zoo trade. It is now illegal to capture wild orangutans for export to zoos or private collectors.

The zoo population of orangutans is stable, with 170 zoos around the world holding more than 850 animals. Several second-generation births have occurred in zoos, and the captive population is believed to be in good shape.

Primate Conservation

The numbers of primates in the wild are decreasing. Primate conservation includes protection of both the animals and their habitats.

Why primates are in trouble • Most of the primates of the world are found in tropical rain forests. Tropical rain forests cover only seven percent of the earth's surface, yet 40 percent of the earth's creatures are found there. In other words, nearly half of the earth's plants and animals are found on less than ten percent of the land.

It took 75 million years for the tropical rain forests to form, and in the last 200 years nearly half of these irreplaceable forests have disappeared. It is estimated that we are altering tropical rain forests at a rate of 80,000 square miles (207,200 square kilometers) a year; this is equivalent in size to the states of Ohio and Indiana.

Currently, there are more than five billion people on earth, and our population is increasing by nearly 100 million every year. At this rate, the world's human population will double by the year 2050. In less developed nations (where most of the primates are found), it is estimated that the population will double much sooner than this.

Where will human beings find food and shelter in the coming years?

In the United States, when we need food we go to the grocery store. When we need wood to build our houses, we go to the lumberyard. Many tropical countries do not have these luxuries. To survive, the people are forced to hunt the animals that live in the jungle and to cut down trees for fuel and building material. In addition, the governments of these poor nations allow foreign corporations to cut down the forests and set up huge cattle and farming operations. These operations provide little food and very few jobs for the people that live in the forest.

Although the jungle looks lush and fertile, it is actually very fragile. The nutrients for the soil are provided by the decomposition of dead leaves and rotting logs. When the trees are gone, the soil dies, and all that's left is barren ground. A section of tropical jungle, "clear-cut" for farming or grazing, will last less than five years. When the cultivated land is worn out, the farmer or rancher simply moves farther into the jungle, slashing and burning and creating more land for ranching and farming.

Most of the meat raised on tropical land is exported to wealthy nations that can afford to pay high prices for it. This means that the people living in the tropics generally must get their protein by hunting and trapping the animals that live in the jungle.

Primates are a common item in the diets of tropical peoples. Primate meat is also used for bait, to catch fish, turtles, and other animals. Primate bones, teeth, and skulls are made into necklaces and sold to tourists. Primate skin is tanned and made into horse bridles. In South America, the boiled hair of the howler monkey is thought to be able to cure a cough.

In many countries, there are laws to protect primates from this kind of activity. But these laws are difficult to enforce because primates are found in such remote regions of the world.

Another reason primates are in trouble is the pet trade. In the United States it is now illegal to import primates as pets, but some are still imported illegally. Primates are wild animals and make terrible pets. Often the people who keep primates as pets do not feed them the right kinds of foods. The animals are also kept isolated, resulting in behavioral problems.

The importation of primates for laboratory research has declined dramatically during the last ten years, but worldwide, thousands of primates are still imported for this purpose. Many primate research centers are breeding their own primates and putting them in large natural enclosures to study their behavior, which can ultimately contribute to saving species in the wild. But some primates are still being used in medical experiments and are killed during or after the experiment is over. It is hoped that in the future alternative ways can be found to advance scientific knowledge.

All of these things contribute to the decline of primates worldwide. To reverse the trend, conservationists, zoologists, and ecologists are fighting to protect not only the individual primates but also the land on which they live.

Primate conservation in the zoo ark • The zoo ark consists of zoos from all over the world working in cooperation to save animals from extinction. Zoos no longer consider themselves the owners of the animals they house but the custodians. As custodians, their responsibility is to manage each animal in such a way that the entire species benefits.

Many animals in zoos are managed under a program called the *Species Survival Plan*. Animals from various zoos managed under the Species Survival Plan are treated as a single group rather than individually by each zoo. Thus, management decisions can be made that will benefit the whole species (wild and captive) rather than just the individual animal.

One of the main tools of the Species Survival Plan is the *studbook*. Each animal in the program is assigned a studbook number. By looking up the animal's number, a keeper can learn whether the animal was captured in the wild or born in captivity, who its parents are, its date of birth, and its current location. With this information keepers can decide which animals should be bred to improve the overall captive population.

One primate managed under the Species Survival Plan is the golden lion tamarin. This animal is found primarily in a small, protected jungle in Brazil, not far from the city of Rio de Janeiro. With their striking orange-gold fur and large, dramatic mane of hair, golden lion tamarins are considered by many to be the most beautiful primates in the marmoset family.

In 1968 it was discovered that their habitat had dwindled from 8,000 square miles (20,720 square kilometers) to a mere 80 square miles (207 square kilometers) and that there were only 200 golden lion tamarins left in the wild. There were fewer than 100 in zoos. In addition, many of the golden lion tamarins in zoos were found to be suffering from severe vitamin deficiencies and were dying from viral and bacterial infections. By 1972, the captive population of golden lion tamarins had fallen to fewer than 70 animals.

Zoos that had these beautiful creatures banded together to try to improve the health and increase the size of the captive population. Originally, it was thought that golden lion tamarins subsisted mainly on fruits, but it was discovered that these primates also need a great deal of protein in their diet. In addition to this, most animals can get by with ordinary vitamin D, but South American monkeys must have a special type of vitamin D to survive. With improvements in the management of the golden lion tamarins, the captive population began to increase. By 1984 there were almost 400 in zoos—double the population in the wild—and every year the zoo population was increasing by at least 50 animals.

At the same time, a portion of their habitat in Brazil was turned into a preserve and thus protected from further destruction. With this small part of their former habitat secure, and a "surplus" of captive animals, biologists from Brazil and the

Zoos worked together to protect the golden lion tamarin from extinction.

United States began to reintroduce golden lion tamarins back into the wild.

The reintroduction program has been very successful. Since 1984, some 90 animals have been released. These golden lion tamarins have added more than 70 animals to the wild population, increasing it by 25 percent.

Because of all the media attention the reintroduction of tamarins received in South America, the golden lion tamarin is now what is known as a *flagship* species. Posters of the golden lion tamarin and other marmosets have been put up all over Brazil. When people see a picture of the golden lion tamarin, they are reminded of all the unique wildlife their jungle habitat holds, and this gives them a sense of pride. It also helps the local people to become concerned about other animals that share their jungle habitat.

It is too early to tell whether the golden lion tamarin will be saved from extinction. But the signs are encouraging.

Successful animal reintroductions are rare. Unfortunately, there is not enough suitable habitat and it is sometimes difficult to get governments and local people to cooperate in reintroduction programs.

How you can help primates • Over many millions of years, the primates of the world have evolved strategies to protect themselves from predators. Many of them live in trees where they cannot be reached. Some live in large groups, where there is strength in numbers. Others have developed speed so they cannot easily be caught.

But there is no defense against people and habitat destruction. A primate cannot move faster than a bullet or an arrow. It cannot always avoid the snares and traps set by its more intelligent relative, the human primate. And it cannot survive in a habitat that no longer provides it with what it needs to live.

One way to help the primates of the world is to protect the habitat in which they live. This can be done by creating wildlife preserves and parks where it is illegal to injure or kill the animals. Another way to help protect their habitat is to make sure that the meat you buy and eat does not come from a tropical rain forest. Ask at your local butcher shop, supermarket, and restaurant where they get their meat. If they say they don't know or that it is imported, don't buy it! This meat should be available to the people living in the tropics so they don't have to rely on the animals in the jungle for protein. In addition, refusing to eat meat from the tropics helps save primate habitat.

Another thing you can do is to support your local zoo and its programs to preserve animals. The average zoo takes up less than 55 acres (22 hectares). If we were to put all the zoos together, there would be less than 31 square miles (80 square kilometers) of captive habitat. A zoo cannot produce more animals than it can hold. Many zoos are trying to increase the amount of space they have for endangered animals by buying

A hand-reared mandrill baboon "socializes"
with a zookeeper. Mandrill baboons may
become an endangered species in the future.

large tracts of land to be used as captive breeding facilities. You can also help by volunteering your time and helping zoos raise money for wildlife conservation. You can join and support organizations whose primary goal is to preserve the world's dwindling habitats.

In a way, you have already helped a little to save primates from extinction by reading this book. But understanding the problem is only part of the solution. You need to share what you have learned with your family, friends, and classmates. The more people are aware of a problem, the better chance there is of finding a solution.

You and your friends and classmates can write letters to local politicians, telling them of your concerns and asking them what they are doing to solve the problem. You can also write to the leaders of tropical nations.

You may think that the problems of extinction and habitat loss belong to someone else, or that someone else will take care of them. But these problems are shared by all of us living on the earth.

The earth is changed by what
You
Know, say, and do

The fate of the world is up to
You

Glossary

Brachiation. The act of swinging by the arms from branch to branch.

Conservation. The controlled use and protection of natural resources such as trees, land, water, and animals.

Deforestation. The removal of trees from forest and jungle habitat.

Endangered species. An animal that does not have enough of its kind left to maintain or increase its population.

Extinction. What happens when the last animal of a species dies.

Flagship species. A well-known endangered animal, such as a giant panda or golden lion tamarin, that is used to represent the problems facing less well-known endangered animals.

Gestation period. The period of time a female carries her offspring in the uterus before birth.

Imprinting. A process that happens early in the life of any social animal, whereby it learns behavior patterns from its parents, or, in the case of hand-reared animals, from the humans raising it.

Nocturnal animal. An animal that sleeps during the day and is active at night.

Nonverbal communication. The act of communicating without words.

Poaching. The illegal killing of animals.

Primate. The animal classification that includes monkeys and apes.

Prosimian. The classification of monkeys that includes lemurs, lorises, and tarsiers.

Quarantine. A period of time that an animal is kept apart from other animals to make sure that it is not carrying any contagious disease.

Reintroduction. When an endangered animal is bred in a zoo and released back into its natural habitat.

Second-generation birth. When the first offspring of wild-born animals produce offspring of their own in zoos.

Social hierarchy. The ranking order of any social animal group. An animal's rank in the hierarchy is determined by strength, age, leadership abilities, intelligence, sex, and other factors.

Species Survival Plan. An animal conservation plan whereby animal species, such as orangutans, are managed as a single group, regardless of which zoo is keeping them.

Studbook. A species record that tells who an individual animal's parents are, its date of birth, and its sex. The studbook is used by zoologists to pick animal pairs for breeding.

Further Reading

Fossey, Dian. *Gorillas in the Mist*. Boston: Houghton Mifflin, 1983.

Goodall, Jane. *In the Shadow of Man*. Boston: Houghton Mifflin, 1971.

———— *Through a Window: My Thirty Years with the Chimpanzees of Gombe*. Boston: Houghton Mifflin, 1990.

Macdonald, Julie. *Almost Human: The Baboon Wild and Tame—in Fact and Legend*. Radnor, PA: Chilton Books, 1965.

MacKinnon, John. *The Ape Within Us*. Orlando, FL: Holt, Rinehart and Winston, 1978.

———— *In Search of the Red Ape*. Orlando, FL: Holt, Rinehart and Winston, 1978.

Mowat, Farley. *Women in the Mists: The Story of Dian Fossey and the Mountain Gorillas of Africa*. New York: Warner Books, 1987.

Napier, J. R., and P. H. Napier. *The Natural History of Primates*. Cambridge, MA: The MIT Press, 1985.

Peterson, Dale. *The Deluge and the Ark: A Journey into Primate Worlds*. Boston: Houghton Mifflin, 1989.

Sanderson, Ivan. *The Monkey Kingdom: An Introduction to Primates*. Radnor, PA: Chilton Books, 1963.

Schultz, Adolph H. *The Life of Primates*. New York: Universe Books, 1969.

Strum, Shirley C. *Almost Human: A Journey into the World of Baboons*. New York: Random House, 1987.

Index